WHITE WOLVES

YEAR

4

C000149705

Stories That Raise Issues

KARINA LAW

A & C Black • London

Contents

White Wolves Series Consultant: Sue Ellis, Centre for Literacy in Primary Education

Reprinted 2008
First published 2006 by
A & C Black Publishers Ltd
38 Soho Square, London, W1D 3HB
www.acblack.com

Text copyright © 2006 Karina Law
Illustrations copyright © 2006 Jane Cope, Cherry Whytock and Pam Smy

The right of Karina Law to be identified as author and the rights of Jane Cope, Cherry Whytock and Pam Smy to be identified as the illustrators of this work have been asserted by them in accordance with the Copyrights, Designs and Patents Act 1988.

ISBN 978-0-7136-7682-2

A CIP catalogue for this book is available from the British Library.

This book is produced using paper that is made from wood grown in managed, sustainable forests. It is natural, renewable and recyclable. The logging and manufacturing processes conform to the environmental regulations of the country of origin.

Printed in Great Britain by Martins the Printers, Berwick upon Tweed.

Introduction

What is Guided Reading?

Guided Reading is a valuable part of literacy work within the classroom, bridging the gap between shared and independent reading. A teacher usually works with a small group of children, who are of similar reading abilities, using a text that has been carefully selected to match the reading ability of the group.

The group setting naturally leads to discussion about the book. The teacher's role is to support pupils in their reading and discussion, and encourage them to respond to the text in a variety of different ways, including personal response. In Guided Reading children can put into practice the reading strategies that have been taught during Shared Reading sessions, and the teacher can monitor their progress more closely.

Aims of Guided Reading

With careful organisation and selection of appropriate texts, Guided Reading can:
- improve reading fluency;
- inspire confidence and promote enjoyment of reading;
- deepen understanding of texts;
- provide an opportunity for purposeful discussion, both teacher-led and spontaneous;
- provide a context for focused talk and listening, including role-play and drama activities;
- offer a stimulus for independent writing;
- provide an opportunity for the teacher to monitor the progress of individual children.

The main aim of Guided Reading sessions is to help children become independent readers.

Assessment

Guided Reading is an excellent opportunity to observe and assess the reading strategies used by individual children. When listening to individual children reading aloud, check for accuracy, fluency and understanding, and note the strategies they use to make sense of less familiar words.

The photocopiable record card on p. 42 may be used to record your observations about individual pupils within each group, noting particular strengths and needs. These observations may be used to help note progression and inform your assessment of children's reading development.

Ongoing assessment will also help you to identify when Guided Reading groups need to be reorganised. Children progress at different rates; those who are progressing more rapidly may benefit from reading more challenging texts, while children who are struggling may need opportunites to read more supportive texts.

How to organise Guided Reading

Many teachers find it helpful to organise daily, dedicated Guided Reading sessions to ensure an uninterrupted focus on the group. It works well if each session has a teaching sequence, and the suggestions in this guide offer a structure that you can draw on to make the most of each text and the learning opportunities within them.

Ideally, each group should have a session of Guided Reading every week. Other children in the class can be engaged in a variety of purposeful, independent activities, such as working on an activity relating to a previous Guided Reading session, carrying out reading journals, or paired reading with books of their own choice.

How to Use This Book

Teaching sequences

This guide outlines five teaching sequences to support the use of three Year 4 books with a Guided Reading group:

Taking Flight – for children who are inexperienced readers

Finding Fizz – for children who have an average level of reading ability

Nothing But Trouble – for more experienced readers.

The teaching sequences take into account important elements of reading at Year 4. However, they will need to be adapted to take into consideration the specific needs of individual children within a group to ensure engagement and progress.

The teaching sequences have been planned to be approximately 30 minutes in length, although this will vary depending on how many of the ideas for "Returning to the text" you choose to include.

Independent reading

Each Guided Reading session is likely to be a combination of silent reading, reading aloud and discussion about the text, with the emphasis on reading for meaning. It will be important to hear all children read aloud at some point during the session in order to monitor their progress. However, less-experienced readers will probably need to spend more time reading aloud each session as they are likely to require a higher level of support developing fluency.

Fluency and understanding are both important in reading. Modelling how to read a sentence, with appropriate phrasing and expression, may help children to make sense of the text. Guided Reading offers many opportunities for word and sentence level work but any significant difficulties demonstrated by individual children should be noted on the record card on p. 42 and addressed afterwards so as not to inhibit the group's understanding and enjoyment of the story.

Returning to the text

The questions and prompts in this section may be used to elicit children's understanding of the text. The questions can be asked either during reading or at the end of the chapter. It is not necessary to ask all the questions, as many of these will be covered in discussion arising spontaneously from reading the text. Encourage children to find the relevant parts of the text to support their answers and ask them to give reasons when offering opinions.

Experienced readers require less "literal" questioning and should be encouraged to develop higher order reading skills, for example prediction, inference and deduction.

Additional ideas for exploring the text further include:

- identifying features such as alliteration, similes, compound words, use of italics and capitalisation;
- opportunities for developing prediction skills;
- a range of role-play and drama activities;
- a stimulus for the activity sheet that follows.

It is important that groups have the experience of a reflective conversation about the book and not a "twenty questions" approach to test comprehension.

Next steps

The activity sheets may be used for independent work either in school or as homework. They offer a variety of ways for children to demonstrate their understanding of the stories along with valuable opportunities for writing for different purposes.

Target Statements for Reading

The NLS target statements for reading at Year 4 will help inform your planning for progression in reading.

Word recognition and phonic knowledge:
- Use knowledge of word formation and a more extensive range of prefixes and suffixes to construct the meaning of words in context.

Grammatical awareness:
- Read aloud with intonation and expression taking account of punctuation, e.g. commas, dashes, hyphens.
- Use knowledge of how commas, connectives and full stops are used to join and separate clauses to maintain fluency and understanding when reading.
- Apply knowledge of the different uses of the apostrophe to maintain understanding.

Use of context:
- Understand narrative order and chronology, tracking the passing of time in stories.

Knowing how texts work:
- Understand how chapters and paragraphs are used to collect, order and build up ideas.

Interpretations and response: literary text:
- Identify and discuss issues locating evidence in the text.
- Interpret the effect the choice of language has – to create moods, build tension, etc.
- Identify the use of expressive, descriptive and figurative language in prose and poetry and interpret the effect of the choice of language to create mood, build tension, etc.
- Respond critically to issues raised in stories, locate evidence in text, and explore alternative courses of action and evaluate the author's solution.

Attitude:
- Develop different reading styles for different text types, e.g. sustained silent reading for longer fiction.
- Describe and review own reading habits.
- Take part in peer group discussion on books.

Taking Flight by *Julia Green*

About the book

Grandad's house is Luke's favourite place. He especially loves to visit the pigeon loft at the bottom of the garden and tell the birds his secrets. Then, Grandad falls ill and is taken to hospital. Luke promises to take care of the pigeons for him. Luke talks about the pigeons to his class at school. When he visits Grandad in hospital, Luke tells him about the talk and how interested the other children were. He tells Grandad that the pigeons are missing him. Luke realises Grandad is very sick and is unlikely to get better.

Luke and Mum move in to look after Grandad when he arrives home from hospital. He tells Luke that it will soon be "time to go". Luke carries Grandad's favourite pigeons into the house so that he can say goodbye to them.

When Grandad dies, Luke remembers all the happy times they had together. When he sets the pigeons free for their flight, Luke feels sure that Grandad is still watching him, somehow.

Luke walks home from school. It takes him exactly twelve minutes and fifty seconds. He goes straight to the pigeon loft. His pigeons are waiting for him.

"All right, steady on," he tells them as they push and jostle at the wire. As he unlocks each cage the pigeons hop onto the edge and spread their wings for flight.

Luke watches them. Their silver wings flash in the sunlight as they spiral in the blue sky.

58

59

Taking Flight: Teaching Sequence 1

Summary of Chapter One

Luke is relieved when the school day finally ends and he can go and visit Grandad. Grandad's house is Luke's favourite place. He especially loves to visit the pigeon loft at the bottom of the garden. Luke talks to the birds and tells them secrets. Grandad and Luke let the birds out to fly. They have their tea outside and watch as the birds come back to roost. Luke enjoys being with Grandad so much that he hasn't given a thought to the dirty dishes in the kitchen, or the talk he was supposed to prepare for the next day at school.

Teaching Sequence

Introduction

Talk about the book cover and read the blurb. Ask the children:

- What kind of story do you think this is going to be.
- Do you have a special friend or relation that you like to visit?

Independent reading

Ask the group to read Chapter One, focusing on reading for meaning.

- If necessary, read aloud with expression, to show the sense.
- Discuss less familiar words such as *fossils*, *telescope*, *compass* (p. 11), *preen*, *feathers*, *beady* (p. 13), *arc* (p. 15), *roost* (p. 16).
- Read *pigeon* (p. 12) and discuss how pronouncing this word exactly as it is written (pig-ee-on) may help children remember how to spell it.
- "Mum tuts at Grandad" (p. 16). Children could demonstrate this!

Returning to the text

Develop children's understanding of the story by asking some of these questions either during reading or at the end of the chapter. Encourage the children to find the relevant part in the text to support their answers.

1) Why does Luke let out a big sigh at three o'clock?
2) What does Luke like about visiting Grandad's house? For example: Grandad lets Luke make pancakes; he doesn't ask questions; he doesn't moan or stop him from watching the television; there are interesting things to look at; the garden; the pigeons.
3) Why do you think Luke tells the pigeons his "secrets" (p. 13).
4) Why do you suppose Luke feels different from everybody else at school? (Everybody likes football except for him (p. 13).)
5) How do we know in Chapter One that Grandad is not as fit as he used to be and is less able to look after himself? For example, he walks with a stick now (p. 14), the sink is full of dirty dishes (p. 16) and there is dust everywhere (p. 17).

There are a number of words relating to pigeons in Chapter One. Invite the children to find them and explain their meaning, for example: *pigeon loft*, *feathers*, *peck*, *seed*, *preen*, *coo*, *wings*, *roost* (pp. 12–16).

Talk about the meaning of *ought* (p. 16); think of words that end in *-ought*, for example, *bought*, *brought*, *nought*.

Next steps

The children can now complete Activity Sheet 1: "Luke" which asks them to revisit the text to list all the things they know about Luke.

Luke

Write a list of all the things you have learned about Luke. For example, what are his likes and dislikes? Look at Chapter One again to help you.

- Luke likes to make pancakes at Grandad's house.

- _____

- _____

- _____

- _____

- _____

- _____

- _____

- _____

- _____

- _____

- _____

White Wolves Teachers' Resource
for Guided Reading Year 4
Stories That Raise Issues
© A & C Black 2006

Taking Flight: Teaching Sequence 2

Summary of Chapter Two

Luke listens to the talks given by other children. He is delighted when three o'clock arrives and his teacher announces that the last talks will have to be saved until the next day. He plans to prepare a really good talk about Grandad's pigeons. After school, while Grandad makes pancakes, Luke does the washing-up. Then Grandad has a sleep while Luke feeds the pigeons and lets them out for their fly around. When Grandad wakes, he doesn't look well. Luke telephones his mum who then calls for an ambulance. Grandad stays in hospital overnight and Luke promises to take care of the pigeons for him.

Teaching Sequence

Introduction
Recap on what Chapter One revealed about Luke and Grandad. Ask the children to remind you about the things that Luke enjoyed about his visits to Grandad's house.

Independent reading
Ask the group to read Chapter Two, focusing on reading for meaning.
- Discuss less familiar words, names or phrases such as *enough, highlight, Mira, Marek, dribbling, professionals* (p. 20), *India, sequinned sari, Junior League, goalie, newts* (p. 22), *imagines, listening, maple syrup, sugar* (p. 24), *perch, edge* (p. 25), *veer* (p. 26), *bundled, corridor* (p. 28).

Returning to the text
Develop children's understanding of the story by asking some of these questions either during reading or at the end of the chapter. Encourage them to find the relevant part in the text to support their answers.

1) Why do you think Mum want Luke to go to school rather than stay with Grandad? (She thinks Grandad needs to rest (p. 20).)
2) Can you remember what Mira, Marek and Joe talk about to the class? (Mira talks about attending her aunty's wedding in India, Marek talks about being a goalkeeper in the Junior League and Joe talks about the newts in his garden (p. 22).)
3) Why do you suppose Luke decide to talk about this particular topic?
4) What is Grandad concerned about while he is in hospital? (He asks Luke to take care of the pigeons (p. 30).)

Discuss Luke's handling of the situation in this chapter. How well does he deal with the emergency? How does he show how grown-up and sensible he has become? For example: by doing Grandad's washing-up, looking after the pigeons, making tea, telephoning his mum, keeping Grandad warm and comforted.

Has anyone ever had to deal with an emergency? Invite them to share their experiences and discuss how they handled the situations.

Ask the children to say how each character – Luke, Grandad and Mum – is feeling at the end of the chapter. For example: tired, sad, frightened, lonely (Grandad).

Next steps
The children can now complete Activity Sheet 2: "A Long Day" which asks them to put themselves into Luke's shoes and write a diary account of his day.

A Long Day

Imagine you are Luke. Write a diary account about everything that happened today. Include some of your thoughts and feelings.

It has been a long and difficult day today! When I woke up this morning, I didn't feel well...

_____

_____

_____

After lunch, some of the other children in my class did their talks...

_____

_____

_____

I had pancakes again at Grandad's. Then, while I was doing the washing-up, Grandad fell asleep in his deckchair. He was asleep for ages...

_____

_____

_____

When Grandad woke up he looked strange. I helped him inside and made him a cup of tea...

_____

_____

_____

Grandad was taken to hospital in an ambulance...

_____

_____

_____

Taking Flight: Teaching Sequence 3

Summary of Chapter Three

Luke delivers his talk about pigeons to the class. The other children listen with interest and everyone claps at the end. Joe asks if he can come and see the pigeons. When Luke visits Grandad in hospital he tells him about the talk and how everyone liked it. He tells Grandad that the pigeons are missing him. On the way home, Luke lets the pigeons out and cleans their cages while Mum cleans Grandad's house. Over tea, Mum and Luke talk about Grandad. Luke realises he is very sick and is unlikely to get better.

Teaching Sequence

Introduction

Ask the children, in pairs, to summarise what has happened in the story so far in just three sentences. For example: Luke has been enjoying visiting Grandad after school and helping to look after the pigeons. He has been worrying about what subject to talk about in front of his class; Grandad has been taken ill and is now in hospital.

Independent reading

Ask the group to read Chapter Three, focusing on reading for meaning.

- Discuss less familiar words such as *hopper*, *trough*, *turquoise* (p. 32), *fascinating* (p. 35), *recognise* (p. 36), *beauties* (p. 37), *echoes* (p. 38), *jostling*, *crooing* (p. 39), *unlatches* (p. 40).
- Talk about *homers* (p. 33); explain what a homing pigeon is.

Returning to the text

Develop children's understanding of the story by asking some of these questions either during reading or at the end of the chapter. Encourage them to find the relevant part in the text to support their answers.

1) What need to be done to take care of the pigeons? (Put seed in the hopper, fill the water troughs, let them out to fly, clean the cages with a special brush, sweep out the loft.)

2) How is Grandad when Luke visits him in hospital?

Discuss how Luke feels about giving his talk to the class. Look for evidence in the text that reveals how nervous he is feeling when his turn comes. (His hands are shaking (p. 31), his voice is quiet and a bit shaky.) Why does the talk become easier for Luke once he gets going?

Talk together about how Luke and Mum feel after seeing Grandad and how Luke's mum deals with the situation. What do the children think about her honesty? Would it be better to pretend that Grandad will be fine? How does she reassure Luke? (She holds his hand, a sign that she is there for him, whatever happens (p. 42).) Children may wish to share their experience of losing a loved one.

Discuss the way in which the pigeons help Luke to deal with his troubles. For example: he confides in them his worries about being different from the others in his class; they help him conquer his fear of doing his talk, providing him with an interesting subject; they are a comfort to him when Grandad is in hospital; they take his mind off things when he is busy looking after them.

What would they choose to talk about if they had to give a five-minute talk to the class.

Next steps

The children can now complete Activity Sheet 3: "Pigeon Talk" which provides a format for making notes about keeping pigeons using information from the book. The notes can be used by the children to give a short talk about pigeons themselves.

Pigeon Talk

Imagine you are going to give a short talk about pigeons. Write a few notes under each heading, using information you have read in the book, to help you plan what to say.

Interesting facts about pigeons:

_____

_____

_____

_____

_____

_____

_____

How pigeons look:
● They have bright, beady eyes.

_____

_____

_____

_____

Looking after pigeons:

_____

_____

_____

_____

_____

White Wolves Teachers' Resource
for Guided Reading Year 4
Stories That Raise Issues
© A & C Black 2006

Taking Flight: Teaching Sequence 4

Summary of Chapter Four

On Saturday, Luke looks after the pigeons while Mum finishes cleaning the house. They go to visit Grandad in hospital and discover that he has been moved to his own room. While Mum talks to the nurse, Luke finds Grandad. He doesn't look like Grandad any more. He asks Luke to take him home. Mum agrees and Grandad travels home in an ambulance. Luke and Mum move in with Grandad to look after him. Grandad sleeps most of the time but he is able to see the pigeons when Luke lets them out for a fly around. Grandad tells Luke that it will soon be "time to go". Luke carries Grandad's favourite pigeons into the house so that he can say goodbye to them.

Teaching Sequence

Introduction
Ask each child in the group to recap briefly on a different aspect of the book so far. For example: Luke's relationship with his Grandad, Luke's worries at school, his talk on pigeons, and Grandad becoming ill and being taken into hospital.

Independent reading
Ask the group to read Chapter Four, focusing on reading for meaning.
- Discuss less familiar words such as *panicky* (p. 46), *sunken*, *bony* (p. 47), *blessed*, *glimpse* (p. 50), *nestle*, *flight* (p. 52).
- Mum brings Grandad sweet peas from the garden (p. 48); do the children realise that these are a variety of flowers?

Returning to the text
Develop children's understanding of the story by asking some of these questions either during reading or at the end of the chapter. Encourage them to find the relevant part in the text to support their answers.

1) Why do you think Grandad has been moved out of the hospital ward?
2) Why does the nurse want to have "a private word" with Mum?
3) Why do you think it says: "Grandad doesn't look like Grandad any more"? (Explain that, although Grandad still looks the way he did the week before, he is not looking "himself"; Luke notices changes in him that show he is now very ill.)
4) A tear rolls down Grandad's cheek when he sees Luke (p. 47); is he pleased to see Luke?

Why do you think everyone decided it is best for Grandad to go home, even though he is still very ill. Do you think it is the right decision?

Luke thinks that he and Mum should have moved in with Grandad ages ago but Mum disagrees (p. 50). Ask the group what they think about this.

Grandad tells the pigeons "Time for me to take flight" (p. 52). Talk about what Grandad means by this and note how the phrase "take flight" links back to the title of the book.

The children could role-play different characters from the book engaged in conversation. For example: Luke and Grandad in hospital; Luke's mum talking to the nurse about Grandad; Luke and his mum discussing what Grandad would want.

Next steps
The children can now complete Activity Sheet 4: "Then and Now" which asks them to consider the changes that have taken place as the story has progressed.

Then and Now

Look back at Chapter One. What has changed since the story began? Make a note of the differences between *then* and *now*.

Then	Now
■ Grandad looked after himself.	■ Grandad needs to be looked after.
■ _____	■ _____
■ _____	■ _____
■ _____	■ _____
■ _____	■ _____
■ _____	■ _____
■ _____	■ _____

White Wolves Teachers' Resource
for Guided Reading Year 4
Stories That Raise Issues
© A & C Black 2006

Taking Flight: Teaching Sequence 5

Summary of Chapter Five

Luke wakes in the night and hears Mum talking on the phone. She tells Luke that Grandad has died. Luke and Mum sit and cry together. When Luke returns to bed he remembers all the happy times he has had with Grandad. He dreams about the pigeons; they are carrying Grandad with them as they circle and spiral into the sky. Luke knows that, wherever Grandad is, he is happy and safe now. After the funeral, when Luke returns to school, the other children are friendly towards him. Luke tells Joe that Grandad's pigeons are his now, and that he has moved into Grandad's house with his mum. He invites Joe to come and see the pigeons. When he sets the pigeons free for their flight, Luke feels sure that Grandad is still watching him, somehow.

Teaching Sequence

Introduction
Recap on what has happened in the story so far. How do the children think the story will end?

Independent reading
Ask the group to read Chapter Five, focusing on reading for meaning.
- Discuss less familiar words and phrases such as *spiral* (p. 55), *funeral* (p. 56), *newt spawn* (p. 57), *jostle* (p. 59).

Returning to the text
Develop children's understanding of the story by asking some of these questions either during reading or at the end of the chapter. Encourage them to find the relevant part in the text to support their answers.
1) What does Luke hear when he wakes in the night? (He hears Mum's feet on the stairs and her voice as she talks on the telephone (p. 53).)
2) What does he think about when he returns to bed after learning that Grandad has died? (He remembers all the happy times he has had with Grandad (p. 54) and he dreams about the pigeons carrying Grandad into the sky (p. 55).)
3) How are the other children towards Luke when he returns to school? (They tell Luke that they missed him and invite him to join in their game of football (p. 56).)
4) What do you think Grandad would think about Luke looking after the pigeons?

Ask the children, in pairs, to think about Luke's special memories of his grandfather. How will he remember him?

Discuss how the pigeons have again helped Luke overcome difficulties in his life. For example: They are a comfort to him, helping him to come to terms with the loss of his grandfather; they also help him to make friends with Joe, who is interested in seeing them.

Some children may wish to talk about their special memories of loved ones who have died.

Next steps
The children can use Activity Sheet 5: "Remembering Grandad" to think about and write Luke's special memories of his grandfather. Alternatively, this sheet could be used to record personal memories of a special friend or relative should any child wish to do so. They may choose to bring in a photograph to help them.

Remembering Grandad

Imagine you are Luke.
How will you remember Grandad?
Write your special memories about him here.

_____

_____

_____

_____

_____

_____

_____

_____

_____

_____

_____

_____

White Wolves Teachers' Resource
for Guided Reading Year 4
Stories That Raise Issues
© A & C Black 2006

Finding Fizz by J. Alexander

About the book

Finding Fizz is a story about bullying and being part of a gang. Carly is one of the Funny Five; a group of girls who are always giggling together. But when she wears a skirt to school, Carly is teased about her fat ankles. The teasing continues, however hard Carly tries to ignore it and as the story progresses, it gets much worse.

The discovery of a stray dog takes Carly's mind off the gang and the cruel comments. If anyone is horrible to her, she just thinks about the little dog waiting for her at home and it makes her smile. Then she befriends Maisie, another girl who had been bullied by the gang, and realises how Maisie must have felt. The gang name the two girls the Sisters of Sad but they don't care. A new friendship and the companionship of a little dog were all Carly needed to "find her fizz".

Carly told Maisie that the dog didn't have a name. "We haven't had him very long," she said.

She didn't want to admit that they might not be keeping him very long, either.

"He's got to have a name!" said Maisie.

They talked about names for a bit and then gave up because they couldn't think of a good one. Then they played ball with the dog until he buried it.

46

Lying on the lawn in the sunshine, Carly decided to trust Maisie and tell her the truth. "The trouble is," she said. "The dog isn't really mine. I found him."

"Where?"

"Under the hedge. Mum says if no one comes to claim him before Saturday then we'll know he's been abandoned and I can keep him."

47

Finding Fizz: Teaching Sequence 1

Summary of Chapter One

When Carly wears a skirt to school instead of the usual trousers, her friends tease her about her fat ankles. The teasing gets worse as the day continues, even though Carly tries to ignore it. She is used to being part of a gang – the Funny Five – and feels upset at being left out and called names. Her friends have even drawn a picture of her with tree trunks for legs. On the way home, the teasing continues on the school bus. Carly leaves the bus at the first stop and walks the last mile home. She slips into an alley to calm down before going into her house and it is here that she hears a whimper, like an animal in pain, coming from under the garden hedge.

Teaching Sequence

Introduction
Talk about the book cover and read the blurb. Ask the children:
- What kind of story do you think this is going to be?
- Do you think it will have a happy ending?

Independent reading
Ask the group to read Chapter One, focusing on reading for meaning.
- Read aloud to emphasise the meaning. For example: "Ouch! I think I've got a splinter!" (p. 16); demonstrate with expression how the boy is teasing Carly.
- Discuss less familiar words and phrases such as *blubbing* (p. 9), *so-called* (p. 16), *whimper* (p. 17).

Returning to the text
Develop children's understanding of the story by asking some of these questions either during reading or at the end of the chapter. Encourage them to find the relevant part in the text to support their answers.

1) Why do you think Carly wore a skirt to school? (Jax suggested they should all wear skirts, so they did (p. 7).)
2) How did Carly feel when Jax and the gang made fun of her ankles?
3) Why was Jax's gang known as the Funny Five? (Their teacher, Miss Fenn, gave them the nickname because they were always giggling (p. 8).)
4) How did Jax's gang react when Carly got upset about their teasing?
5) Why did Carly get off the bus at the first stop?
6) What do you think Carly will find in the hedge? (The front cover of the book provides a clue.)

Note the way the author has started this story, launching straight into dialogue and an unkind comment from Jax. What do the group think about this kind of opening?

Ask the children to find a simile on p. 11 (*as thin as a stick*).

Talk about the nicknames referred to in the chapter: *Funny Five*, *Miss Piggy* (p. 8), *Mopey Mo* (p. 9), *crybaby* (p. 13), *Tree trunks* (p. 14). Talk about their meaning and purpose. Which names are friendly and which are intended to hurt or poke fun? The children may like to talk about how they feel when they are called names (without revealing the nicknames or the people who use them).

Discuss gangs in general; consider how nice it feels to be part of a group and how lonely it can feel to be left out.

Next steps
The children can now complete Activity Sheet 1: "Crybaby Carly" which requires them to look at the events of Chapter One through the eyes of another member of Jax's gang.

Crybaby Carly

Imagine you are one of the Funny Five. Write a diary account about what happened at school today.

Think about:
- How Jax behaved towards Carly
- How Carly reacted
- How Carly felt
- Did you join in the teasing? Why?

_____

_____

_____

_____

_____

_____

_____

_____

_____

_____

_____

_____

Finding Fizz: Teaching Sequence 2

Summary of Chapter Two

Carly discovers what is making the whimpering noise: a thin, stray dog, lying under a hedge. She wraps him in her sweatshirt and takes him home. Mum is happy for Carly to look after the dog, at least until his owner can be found.

It seems that Mum has noticed how unhappy Carly is, as has Miss Fenn, Carly's teacher, who has been talking to Mum on the phone. Mum suggests that Carly talks about whatever is bothering her. In the excitement of finding the dog, Carly had forgotten about Jax and the gang. She tells the little dog all about how her friends are treating her and how she thinks they might never let her back into the gang.

Teaching Sequence

Introduction
Ask each child in turn to tell you one thing they learned about Carly and the Funny Five in the first chapter.

Independent reading
Ask the group to read Chapter Two, focusing on reading for meaning.
- Discuss less familiar words and phrases such as *strays* (p. 18), *sausage* (p. 22) – note the smaller word *age* within this word; *blows over* (p. 25).
- What does Carly mean when she says that "Mum didn't go nuts" (p. 20)?

Returning to the text
Develop children's understanding of the story by asking some of these questions either during reading or at the end of the chapter. Encourage them to find the relevant part in the text to support their answers.
1) What condition was the dog in when Carly found him? (He was very thin; you could see his ribs under his fur (p. 19).)

2) Why do you think Carly's mum was not cross when Carly brought home the stray dog?
3) What things did Carly and her mum do to help the dog recover? (They gave him water to drink (p. 20), a cold sausage to eat (p. 22) and left him to sleep.)
4) Why do you think Miss Fenn rang Carly's mum?
5) Why did Carly not want to tell Mum about Jax and the gang? (She thought it was only a bit of teasing and she should be able to handle it by herself (p. 24).)
6) What does Mum mean when she says "It's not a good idea to bottle things up" (p. 24)?

Talk about Mum's advice about approaching stray dogs (p. 18). Why is it not a good idea to stroke a dog you do not know?

Look at the author's description of the dog (p. 19): "His body was so thin she could see the hard ridges of his ribs under the wiry brown fur." What makes this so effective? Can the children visualise the dog easily from it?

We learn from Mum, following a telephone call from Miss Fenn, that Carly's teacher is worried about her and has noticed she is not her "usual happy self" at the moment. Ask the children, in pairs, to role-play the telephone conversation between Mum and Miss Fenn. They could use the opening lines on Activity Sheet 2 to help them get started.

Next steps
The children can now complete Activity Sheet 2: "A Call From Miss Fenn", which asks them to write a short dialogue between Carly's mum and her teacher.

A Call From Miss Fenn

Continue the telelphone conversation between Carly's mum and her teacher, Miss Fenn.

Miss Fenn: Good evening. It's Miss Fenn here, Carly's teacher.

Mum: Hello, Miss Fenn. Is everything OK? Carly's not in any trouble, is she?

Miss Fenn: _____

_____

_____

_____

_____

_____

_____

_____

_____

_____

_____

White Wolves Teachers' Resource
for Guided Reading Year 4
Stories That Raise Issues
© A & C Black 2006

Finding Fizz: Teaching Sequence 3

Summary of Chapter Three

Now that Carly has a dog to care for, she is less bothered about the teasing at school. If anyone is horrible to her, she just thinks about the little dog waiting for her at home and it makes her smile. But on the way home, Carly notices a card that her mum has placed in a shop window, with information about the dog and where to reclaim him. Carly is upset about this and worries that someone will come to take the dog away.

Teaching Sequence

Introduction
Ask the children to summarise what has happened in the story so far in just three sentences.

Independent reading
Ask the group to read Chapter Three, focusing on reading for meaning.
- Discuss less familiar words and phrases such as *ducked* (p. 27), *strength* (p. 29), *fleeting smile* (p. 31), *village* (p. 32) – note the smaller word *age* within this word; *yelp* (p. 33), *convince* (p. 35).

Returning to the text
Develop children's understanding of the story by asking some of these questions either during reading or at the end of the chapter. Encourage them to find the relevant part in the text to support their answers.
1) Was there anything that puzzled you in the story?
2) How did Carly cope with people being horrible to her during the school day? (She thought about the little dog waiting at home for her, which made her smile (p. 28).)
3) What did she have planned for herself and the dog to do?

4) The others told Miss Fenn that Carly was being horrible to them. Why did they say it?
5) Why do you think Miss Fenn suggested that Carly move to another table?
6) Why didn't Carly want to be too friendly towards Maisie at first? (She thought she would never get back into the Funny Five (p. 31).)
7) Why was Carly upset about the notice in the shop window?

Focus on expression. Ask children to role-play the following lines appropriately, using the author's prompts (*hissed; said under her breath; shouted*):
- "Serves her right," Jax hissed. "Now she'll have to sit with Mopey Mo." (p. 30)
- "Losers," Maisie said under her breath, as Carly sat down. "Don't take any notice of them." (p. 30)
- "What have you done?" she shouted at her mother as soon as she opened the door. (p. 33)

Talk about the way that Carly coped with the teasing at school. Ask the children to discuss how they would have handled the situation if they were Carly.

Next steps
The children can now complete Activity Sheet 3: "FOUND" which asks them to write a card for a local shop window about a pet that has been found.

FOUND

Imagine you have found a stray pet. Write and design a card to put in the window of your local shop.

Don't forget:
- Include a description of the pet
- Write where and when it was found
- Include your telephone number
- Draw a picture of the pet

How will Carly feel if the owner of the dog sees the card in the window and comes to claim him?

_____

_____

_____

_____

Summary of Chapter Four

Jax and the gang continue to ignore Carly. She tries to cheer herself up by thinking about the little dog but it doesn't work now. She worries that the dog's owner may have seen Mum's card in the window and might call to take him away before she has had a chance to say goodbye. Meanwhile, Carly befriends Maisie, another girl who has been teased and excluded from the gang. Carly now realises how Maisie must have felt. She invites Maisie to her house after school and they play with the little dog. Carly explains that the dog is not hers but if no one comes to claim him by Saturday she can keep him.

Teaching Sequence

Introduction

Recap on the events of the story so far. Do the group think Jax and her gang will get tired of teasing Carly? Will Carly be invited to join Jax's gang again? Will Carly and Maisie become friends?

Independent reading

Ask the group to read Chapter Four, focusing on reading for meaning.
- Discuss less familiar words such as *hesitated* (p. 39), *realised* (p. 42), *weird, doodles, saddos* (p. 43), *joyfully* (p. 45), *trouble, abandoned* (p. 47).

Returning to the text

Develop children's understanding of the story by asking some of these questions either during reading or at the end of the chapter. Encourage them to find the relevant part in the text to support their answers.
1) What two things are worrying Carly? (The gang are still ignoring her (p. 36) and she is worried that she might lose the dog (p. 37).)

2) Why does Carly stay inside at playtime?
3) What does Carly apologise to Maisie about? (She is sorry that she and the gang were horrible to Maisie (p. 40).)
4) Why had Maisie given up drawing? (Because Jax had said that art was for "saddos" (p. 43).)
5) Do you have any idea why Carly has to wait until Saturday before she can keep the dog?

Look at the sentence: "It didn't feel like a joke any more; it felt really nasty." (p. 38), which marks a turning point in the story. The teasing has not stopped and Carly feels very unhappy. Discuss with the group the signs that the teasing is more than just a bit of harmless fun. For example: both Carly's mum and her teacher noticed that Carly is not her usual, happy self (p. 23); Miss Fenn was concerned enough to phone Carly's mum; Carly walked the last mile home to avoid being teased on the school bus (p. 16); Carly stayed at her desk instead of going outside at playtime (p. 38). Discuss how to recognise when teasing is just a bit of fun and when it has become more serious and something needs to be done. What should Carly do next? Who could she tell?

Talk about the way Carly deals with her unhappiness in this chapter. For example: she tries to cheer herself up by thinking about the dog (p. 37); she avoids the children who are teasing her by staying inside at playtime (p. 38); she makes friends with Maisie, who knows exactly what she is going through.

Next steps

The children can now complete Activity Sheet 4: "Ups and Downs" which asks them to reflect on different events in the story, from Carly's perspective.

Ups and Downs

Carly's feelings change at different stages in the story. How does she feel in each of these situations? Use words from the book to support your answers.

In class:
Carly forced herself to laugh with the children who made fun of her in class but she must have felt embarrassed because her face turned red…

_____

_____

_____

_____

On the bus:

_____

_____

_____

_____

_____

Finding a friend:

_____

_____

_____

_____

_____

Ignoring the gang:

_____

_____

_____

_____

_____

_____

_____

_____

White Wolves Teachers' Resource
for Guided Reading Year 4
Stories That Raise Issues
© A & C Black 2006

Finding Fizz: Teaching Sequence 5

Summary of Chapter Five

The gang name Carly and Maisie the Sisters of Sad but they don't care. And when Jax invites Carly to a sleepover, Carly declines. Instead, on Saturday, she takes her little dog to the park to meet Maisie. She discovers Maisie with an art class, sketching skateboarders for a comic strip. Maisie started the art classes when she was being teased. They cheered her up and helped her "find her fizz" again. Carly realises that the little dog has helped her to "find her fizz", too. And so the perfect name is found for the stray dog: Fizz!

Teaching Sequence

Introduction

Ask the children to summarise what has happened in the story so far. Give them five minutes to discuss, in pairs, how they think the story might end.

Independent reading

Ask the group to read Chapter Five, focusing on reading for meaning.

- Discuss less familiar words and phrases such as *gratefully, wet kipper, knocked back* (p. 51), *sketchbooks* (p. 54), *launched* (p. 55), *kiosk* (p. 57).

Returning to the text

Develop children's understanding of the story by asking some of these questions either during reading or at the end of the chapter. Encourage them to find the relevant part in the text to support their answers.

1) How did Carly react when the gang called her and Maisie the Sisters of Sad? (She didn't care; all she could think about was her dog and the prospect of losing him (p. 50).)

2) Why do you think Jax decided to invite Carly to a sleepover?

3) How did Jax react when Carly said she was doing something else that day?

4) Why had Maisie joined the art class? (To cheer herself up when Jax and the gang were being horrible to her (p. 57).)

Discuss what Carly means when she says to Maisie: "That's how you found your fizz." (p. 58). Talk about how this links back to the title of the book. How did Carly find her fizz?

Ask the children to discuss their favourite bit in this chapter. For example: when Carly turned down Jax's invitation. What was their favourite part in the book as a whole? Did they think that Carly handled the teasing well? What might she have done differently? What would they have done in Carly's situation?

Ask the children to act out, in pairs, the conversation between Jax and Carly when Jax invited Carly to a sleepover and was turned down.

Next steps

The children can use Activity Sheet 5: "Finding Fizz" to reflect on the things they like to do to cheer themselves up.

Finding Fizz

Carly found her fizz when she found the little dog under the hedge. Just thinking about him waiting for her at home made her smile.

Art classes are Maisie's favourite thing in the world.

What do you like to do to cheer yourself up whenever you have "lost your fizz"?

My favourite thing in the world is _____

_____

_____

_____

_____

_____

_____

_____

_____

_____

_____

White Wolves Teachers' Resource
for Guided Reading Year 4
Stories That Raise Issues
© A & C Black 2006

Nothing But Trouble
by *Alan MacDonald*

About the book

Nothing But Trouble is about not fitting in. The story follows the developing friendship between Paul and the new boy at his school, Jago. It explores the prejudice that Jago faces as one of a family of travellers. Paul has been selected to help Jago settle into his new school. It's not an easy task as, to begin with, Jago says very little and doesn't seem interested in making friends. To complicate things further, Paul's best friend, Sean, is not keen on Jago. However, when Paul discovers Jago's secret – keeping watch over a family of foxes – the two boys develop a special bond. Jago begins to trust Paul and the foxes gradually learn to trust the two boys. Trouble starts, however, when fights and disagreements break out between Sean and Jago, and Paul finds himself stuck in the middle of his two friends. In the end, Paul has to say goodbye to the foxes and Jago as both are forced to move on.

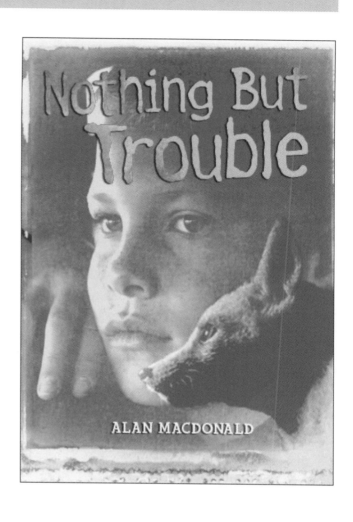

ALAN MACDONALD

Chapter Two

The next day was just as hard work as the first. It wasn't that Jago was mean or spiteful to anyone. He just didn't say much. Even at lunch he just bent over his plate and shovelled the food into his mouth without a word. That day it was stir-fry chicken and rice, which is one my favourites.

Half-way through the meal, I noticed Jago do something odd.

16

He had hardly touched his chicken, leaving it on one side of the plate. But when he thought no one was looking, he slipped it into a plastic bag. The bag went into his pocket. Glancing up, he caught me staring at him.

"What's that for?" I asked.

"Nothing. I'm keeping it for later."

17

Nothing But Trouble: Teaching Sequence 1

Summary of Chapter One

Paul remembers the first time he saw the travellers, or "gypsies" as Sean calls them. They were staying in caravans by the river. Sean tells Paul that the "gypsies" are nothing but trouble and warns him not to let them see his bike or they'll be after it. Then a new boy, Jago, arrives at Paul's school and Paul is chosen to be his buddy and help him settle in. Paul is not very enthusiastic about the task as Jago does not have much to say for himself. Jago answers most questions with a shrug but he becomes defensive when Sean asks him if he is "one of them gypsies" and he reacts angrily when Sean makes unkind remarks about him. It looks to Paul as though Jago is going to have trouble fitting in.

Teaching Sequence

Introduction
Talk about the book cover and read the blurb.
Ask the children:
- What kind of story do you think this is going to be?
- Who are the main characters?

Independent reading
Ask the group to read Chapter One, focusing on reading for meaning.
- If necessary, model how to read sentences, with expression, to show the sense.
- Discuss less familiar words and phrases such as *gypsies* (p. 8), *volunteers* (p. 10), *newcomers* (p. 11), *determined, kick-off* (p. 15).
- Who is narrating/telling this story? (Paul.)

Returning to the text
Develop children's understanding of the story by asking some of these questions either during reading or at the end of the chapter. Encourage them to find the relevant part in the text to support their answers.

1) Sean's dad says gypsies are "trouble; they'll steal anything" (p. 8). What do you feel about these comments?
2) What comments does Paul's mum make about the gypsies? (She calls them "travellers" because they move from place to place, never staying long; she says some people don't like them because they leave litter behind (p. 9).)
3) What do you think Paul's opinion of them is?
4) How does Paul feel about being chosen to be Jago's "buddy"?

The author has written this book as if Paul (the narrator) is telling the story out loud. Ask the children to find examples of this informal style, for example: "I was stuck with him... You're meant to look after them, show them where to go – stuff like that." (p. 11).

Talk about Jago's body language in Chapter One. Ask the children to find references in the text and discuss what they suggest about Jago. For example: *Jago scratched his arm* (p. 10), *Jago propped his chin in his hands* (p. 11), *he trailed after Sean and me with his hands in his pockets* (p. 12), *Jago shrugged* (p. 12), *Jago lifted his chin and I saw his fists clench* (p. 13), *He gave another shrug* (p. 13). Why do you think the author has included so much detail about Jago's body language? (Discuss how, because Jago says very little, it is the only clue the reader has about how he is feeling.)

Discuss how newcomers are made to feel welcome in your school. Can the children remember how they felt on their first day?

Next steps
The children can now complete Activity Sheet 1: "The Caravans" which asks them to find the different opinions expressed by characters in the book about the travellers on the riverside.

The Caravans

Read the following extract:

"We came upon the caravans by the river. Smoke was curling from a fire. Outside the caravans people were sitting talking. A few little kids were chasing a barking dog."

How do the different characters in the story view the travellers?

Sean's dad:

_____

_____

_____

Sean:

_____

_____

_____

Paul's mum:

_____

_____

_____

What do you think Paul thinks about the travellers?

_____

_____

_____

White Wolves Teachers' Resource
for Guided Reading Year 4
Stories That Raise Issues
© A & C Black 2006

Nothing But Trouble: Teaching Sequence 2

Summary of Chapter Two

Paul finds it difficult being Jago's "buddy" because Jago does not have much to say for himself. Then he notices Jago behaving in an odd way, slipping chicken from his plate into a bag. When he asks what the chicken is for, Jago tells him he is keeping it for later. Paul decides to follow Jago after school to see what he does with the chicken scraps. Jago notices him and responds angrily at first but then bursts out laughing. Finally, he decides to trust Paul and let him in on the secret. He takes him to a deserted house with an overgrown garden, puts the chicken scraps on the ground and gestures to Paul to wait silently and watch what happens.

Teaching Sequence

Introduction
Recap on the events of Chapter One and the main characters: Paul, Jago and Sean. Do the group think that the three boys will become friends in time?

Independent reading
Ask the group to read Chapter Two, focusing on reading for meaning.
- Discuss less familiar words and phrases, such as *shovelled*, *stir-fry* (p. 16), *denying* (p. 20), *curiosity*, *involve*, *sauntered* (p. 22).

Returning to the text
Develop children's understanding of the story by asking some of these questions either during reading or at the end of the chapter. Encourage them to find the relevant part in the text to support their answers.
1) What did Paul find difficult about being Jago's "buddy"? (He is uncommunicative: "He just didn't say much" (p. 16).)
2) What did Jago do that Paul found odd? (He slipped some chicken from his plate into a bag (p. 17).)
3) Why do you think Paul followed Jago after school? (To see what he did with the chicken scraps (pp. 18 and 19).)
4) How did Jago respond when Paul explained why he was following him? (He seemed cross at first but then he burst out laughing. He decided to let Paul in on the secret (p. 21).)

Discuss some of the author's interesting vocabulary choices, for example, *sauntered* (p. 22). The author could simply have said "He walked down the drive" but this would have been less interesting. Ask children to find other examples of interesting word choices.

Jago makes Paul promise he will keep the secret to himself (p. 21). Talk about secrets in general. When is it OK to keep a secret and when is it not? (Children should be aware that they should never be persuaded to keep secret something which makes them feel unhappy, something that feels wrong, or something that could be dangerous.)

Re-read the description of the garden at the bottom of p. 23. Ask the children to spot the adjectives the author has used to help the reader visualise the garden, for example: *broken*, *old*, *wooden*, *thick*.

Next steps
The children can now complete Activity Sheet 2: "Descriptions" which gives children an opportunity to experiment with adjectives of their own in short extracts from the text.

Descriptions

Authors spend a lot of time selecting the best words for describing people and places in stories. Choose adjectives (describing words) of your own to complete the following descriptions from the book.

The following Monday, a new boy turned up at our school...

He was _____ and _____ with

_____, _____ eyes under a tangle of hair.

Jago led me along Churchill Street to a house with _____ windows and nettles growing in the front...

The back garden had a _____ fence, an _____,

_____ shed and was overgrown with weeds. At the bottom,

a _____ jungle of bushes had grown up.

Compare your word choices with those used by the author in the book.

Write a descriptive paragraph of your own. Think of an interesting person or place to describe.

_____

_____

_____

_____

_____

_____

White Wolves Teachers' Resource
for Guided Reading Year 4
Stories That Raise Issues
© A & C Black 2006

Nothing But Trouble: Teaching Sequence 3

Summary of Chapter Three

Paul feels concerned about hiding in someone else's garden but he does not want Jago to think he's scared. Eventually, there is a rustle of leaves and two hungry foxes appear. They eat the meat that Jago has put out for them before slinking back into the bushes. The boys meet there again the next day and continue to do so over the following weeks. The foxes learn to trust them more and more until a cub takes meat from the palm of Jago's hand. The more Paul gets to know Jago, the more he begins to like him. But there is a problem – Sean. He does not like Jago and wants to know why Paul "puts up with him". Increasingly, Paul finds himself stuck in the middle of his two friends.

Teaching Sequence

Introduction
Ask the children to recap on the cliffhanger at the end of Chapter Two. What do they think Jago's secret is? What are he and Paul about to see?

Independent reading
Ask the group to read Chapter Three, focusing on reading for meaning.
- Discuss less familiar words and phrases such as *rustle*, *padding* (p. 25), *vixen* (p. 26), *slunk* (p. 27), *balancing*, *tightrope* (p. 28), *dozen* (p. 29), *palm* (p. 31), *fidget* (p. 32), *needling* (p. 36).
- Talk about some of the expressions and their meanings, for example: "still as the grave", "turned tail", "on its heels" (p. 32); "He gives me the creeps" (p. 35). Which of these expressions is also a simile?

Returning to the text
Develop children's understanding of the story by asking some of these questions either during reading or at the end of the chapter. Encourage them to find the relevant part in the text to support their answers.

1) How did Paul feel about hiding in someone else's garden? (He says it felt wrong but he didn't want Jago to think he was scared (p. 25).)
2) Why do you think the foxes are lean and painfully thin? (This question is not answered specifically in the text although the answer can be deduced from the information on p. 27. The foxes live in a town, where food is less available than it would be to a fox living in the countryside. Aside from the odd mouse or bird, they depend on stealing scraps from humans (p. 27).)
3) Why did Paul and Jago watch the foxes in silence?
4) How did Paul feel about Jago sharing his secret with him?
5) How does Sean feel about the friendship between Paul and Jago?

Look at some of the author's word choices. For example: *glanced* rather than *looked*; *padding* rather than *walking* or *creeping* (p. 25). Ask the children to find other examples that they find interesting.

Look again at the description of the fox: *lean and watchful, eyes black as coal* (pp. 25–26); what do the children think of this description and simile?

Talk about the element of trust in this story. Jago decided to trust Paul in the same way that the foxes learned to trust the boys. Trust was built up slowly over a period of time.

Next steps
The children can now complete Activity Sheet 3: "Paul's Thoughts" which asks them to reflect on Paul's thoughts and feelings at different stages in the story.

Paul's Thoughts

By using Paul as the narrator of this story, the author is able to reveal Paul's thoughts and feelings at different stages.

Write how Paul feels at different times in the story.

When he was chosen to be Jago's buddy:

_____

_____

_____

_____

_____

When he and Jago hid in someone else's garden:

_____

_____

_____

_____

_____

When Jago chose to share his secret with Paul:

_____

_____

_____

_____

_____

When he gets stuck in the middle with his friends hating the sight of each other:

_____

_____

_____

_____

_____

_____

White Wolves Teachers' Resource
for Guided Reading Year 4
Stories That Raise Issues
© A & C Black 2006

Nothing But Trouble: Teaching Sequence 4

Summary of Chapter Four

Things finally come to a head when a school trip is arranged. Paul finds Sean in the cloakroom looking for money for the trip, which he believed he put there that morning. He accuses Jago of taking the money. Jago reacts angrily and Sean pushes him against a wall. Jago fights back, wrestling Sean to the ground and the two boys are sent to the head teacher. Paul has an opportunity to stick by his best friend, Sean, when his teacher asks him what happened, but Paul does not come to his rescue because, if anything, it was Sean who started the fight.

Teaching Sequence

Introduction
Reflect on the events of Chapter Three. Ask the group if they think the three boys will ever become friends.

Independent reading
Ask the group to read Chapter Four, focusing on reading for meaning.

- Discuss less familiar words such as *rummaging* (p. 38), *pleaded* (p. 41), *bonkers* (p. 42), *wildcat*, *wrestled*, *commotion* (p. 44), *bystanders* (p. 46), *hesitated* (p. 49), *suspicious* (p. 50).
- Re-read the sentence starting "Jago's eyes blazed…" (p. 47); what does the author mean by this?

Returning to the text
Develop children's understanding of the story by asking some of these questions either during reading or at the end of the chapter. Encourage them to find the relevant part in the text to support their answers.

1) What is Sean looking for in his school bag? (Money for the trip to Sea Life (p. 39).)
2) Where does Paul suggest the money could be?

(He suggests Sean may have left it at home (p. 39).)
3) Why does Sean believe Jago has taken the money? (We already learned in the previous chapter that Sean thinks a "gypsy" and a thief are the same thing (p. 36). In Chapter Four he tells Jago, "You're a thief like all your lot." (p. 42).)
4) How does Jago react when he is accused of stealing?
5) Who started the fight? (Sean provoked Jago by accusing him of theft and then pushed him hard against a wall (p. 43).)
6) How does Paul respond when Miss Nichols asks him if he saw what happened? Why does he not stick by Sean?

What is "Dunno" (p. 41) short for? Talk about the acceptable use of this "word" here, where it is spoken by Sean; explain that it would not be an appropriate word to use in, for example, a formal letter.

Ask the children to find a simile on p. 46 (*they scattered like a flock of sparrows*).

Ask the children to discuss, in pairs, what they think happened to Sean's money. Was it stolen? Did Jago take it? Or did Sean lose it or simply leave it at home as Paul suggested?

The children could role-play, in groups of three, the meeting between Jago, Sean and the head teacher following the fight in the cloakroom.

Next steps
The children can now complete Activity Sheet 4: "Trouble" which requires them to consider different viewpoints about the fight in the cloakroom.

Trouble

Write a short account of the commotion in the cloakroom, in the words of each of these characters.

Sean
I remember putting the money in the pocket of my bag where I thought it would be safe…

_____

_____

_____

_____

Jago

_____

_____

_____

_____

Paul

_____

_____

_____

_____

White Wolves Teachers' Resource
for Guided Reading Year 4
Stories That Raise Issues
© A & C Black 2006

Nothing But Trouble: Teaching Sequence 5

Summary of Chapter Five

That evening, Paul meets Jago as usual. They decide to go and see the foxes but they discover workmen clearing the garden of nettles and brambles. Jago tells them about the foxes living there but the workmen are unsympathetic. They make it clear that they would happily kill any foxes they see because they are vermin. Jago reacts angrily and one of the workmen threatens him and chases the boys away. Paul then learns that Jago is also being forced to move away as the Council have said that the travellers have to move on. Jago thanks Paul for being his "buddy" at school. Just after waving goodbye, Paul spots two foxes in the grass ahead of him. He considers how, just like Jago, the foxes will be forever moving on.

Teaching Sequence

Introduction
Ask the children to summarise what has happened in the story so far. How do they think the story will end?

Independent reading
Ask the group to read Chapter Five, focusing on reading for meaning.
- Discuss less familiar words and phrases such as *prowling, lecture, not fussed* (p. 52), *plume, peering* (p. 53), *buzzing machine* (an electric hedge-trimmer), *stubble* (p. 54), *devils, vermin* (p. 55), *clout, private property* (p. 56), *allotments, dismay, Council* (p. 58).

Returning to the Text
Develop children's understanding of the story by asking some of these questions either during reading or at the end of the chapter. Encourage them to find the relevant part in the text to support their answers.

1) Paul wondered whether Jago would be waiting for him at the corner of Denman Road as usual. Why was this?
2) How does Jago feel about not going on the school trip? (He says he is "not fussed" and he "wasn't going anyway" (p. 52). The reason for this is unclear until the end of the chapter when we learn that Jago and the other travellers are moving on.)
3) What are the workmen doing in the garden where the foxes are living?
4) How do they respond when Jago tells them there are foxes living there?
5) Why are the travellers moving away? (The Council have instructed them to move on (p. 58).)
6) How does Paul feel about Jago leaving?

Look at some of the descriptions in Chapter Five. For example, the details that indicate the house is no longer empty: "The FOR SALE sign was missing from the front garden and a plume of grey smoke rose from the backyard" (p. 53). Compare the busy, noisy garden scene described on p. 54 with the deserted, silent scene described earlier in the book on p. 23.

Draw comparisons between the foxes and Jago. For example: both have trouble fitting in and are not generally welcomed into their communities; both are slow to trust in the people around them as they have grown fearful of others; both are considered to be trouble (Jago by Sean and his father; the foxes by the workmen); both have no permanent home and are always on the move.

Ask the children to reflect on the title: *Nothing But Trouble*. To whom do they think this title refers?

Next steps
The children can use Activity Sheet 5: "Cover Story" to design a new cover for the story.

Cover Story

Design a new front cover for this story.
- ● Think carefully about which aspect of the story you will illustrate.
- ● Remember to include the name of the author.

Write a short summary of the story or "blurb" to appear on the back cover of the book. Explain briefly what the story is about without giving too much away!

_____

_____

_____

_____

_____

_____

_____

White Wolves Teachers' Resource
for Guided Reading Year 4
Stories That Raise Issues
© A & C Black 2006

Record Card

Group:	Book:

Focus for Session:

Names	Comments

Record Card

The White Wolves Interview: **Julia Green**

About the author

Julia Green writes mainly for young adults. *Blue Moon*, *Baby Blue* and *Hunter's Heart* are all published by Puffin. She lives in Bath with her two teenage children, and lectures in creative writing at Bath Spa University. She is programme leader for the MA in Writing for Young People. She also runs writing workshops for young people and adults.

Who did you like to visit when you were a child and what was special about them?

I liked going to visit my grandpa, grandma and auntie because of the lovely garden near the Sussex Downs, and because they had television (we didn't when I was a child)! I loved the train journey, too: on the way back we'd count the rabbits in the fields. Another favourite visit was to Miss Virgo's bookshop – books from floor to ceiling and even in piles up the stairs.

Where do you find ideas for your stories?

Ideas come from in my head, but they get there from everything around – places, people, memories, things I've done or read or heard about, radio, television, conversations. Then a sort of magic happens, and the muddle of ideas starts to take a different shape and I can feel a story tugging at me…

Describe the place where you write your books.

I write in notebooks, which I carry around. I love writing in cafes, or outside, near the sea. The next stage happens on the laptop, mainly on the dining-room table, or in my attic room, or at the kitchen table if my children are out! I like being able to look out over the allotment to the fields and hills. I don't live in the countryside, but the view from my house makes it seem like I do.

If you were not a writer, what other career might you have chosen?

I've always done other jobs as well as writing. At the moment I teach creative writing at university. I also love leading writing workshops for children. I worked in a medical library once, and in publishing, twice, and I've done lots of teaching jobs. But writing is what I most love, and there isn't any other career I'd want! Perhaps artist or musician – if I had enough talent!

The White Wolves Interview: **J. Alexander**

About the author

Jen Alexander grew up in London but she always wanted to live by the sea, so she moved first to the Shetland Isles and then to North Cornwall, where she lives today.

Jen started writing about 12 years ago, when the youngest of her four children started school. She has written loads of books, both fiction and non fiction, for readers of every age, but she enjoys writing for juniors best!

What do you like to do to cheer yourself up whenever you have "lost your fizz"?
If it's hot, I go to the beach and have a swim in the sea – that never fails! But for the other ten months of the year, I like to lie in a bath full of bubbles and read a good book. It doesn't matter what kind of story it is – funny, exciting, sad or spooky – all kinds of stories can take you out of yourself and make you forget about feeling fed up.

Where do you find ideas for your stories?
Ideas are like daydreams – I don't have to go looking for them, they just arrive. Most daydreams aren't very interesting so you just let them go, but others are really enjoyable or intriguing and you find that you keep coming back to them. That's when the plot starts to thicken…

Describe the place where you write your books.
My study is very small and my table is quite big, so I can't actually shut the door. The pale yellow walls are covered in post-it reminders about things I've got to do, lovely letters from readers, jokes people have told me, pictures of owls and lions and a big calendar with deadlines on it. Every surface is covered with piles of notes, books, gel pens and things I just like looking at, such as the green, plastic pig my daughter gave me for my birthday a few years ago.

If you were not a writer, what other career might you have chosen?
I always wanted to be an artist when I was growing up and that's the only other job I'd really like to try if I were not a writer now.

The White Wolves Interview:
Alan MacDonald

About the author

Alan MacDonald was born in Watford and now lives near the River Trent in Nottingham. At school his ambition was to become a footballer, but then he won a pen in a writing competition and his fate was sealed.

He spent several years in a travelling theatre company before turning full time to writing in 1990. Since then he has published more than 50 books for children, ranging from picture books to novels and non fiction.

Do you remember how you felt when you started a new school?

I remember starting secondary school and finding it all huge and overwhelming. I got in trouble for talking in assembly during my first week.

Where do you find ideas for your stories?

Things often stick in my mind which later come out in a story. In this case we had a couple of foxes in the area where I live. I'd often see them trotting along our back wall and once one of them curled up in the sunshine on our lawn.

Describe the place where you write your books.

I have a top room on the second floor of our house. It has my desk and lots of bookcases and badly needs tidying!

If you were not a writer, what other career might you have chosen?

At school I was sure I was going to be a professional footballer. Now I'd like to be a photographer and travel the world.

White Wolves Resources for Guided Reading

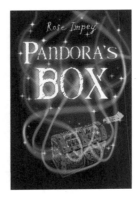

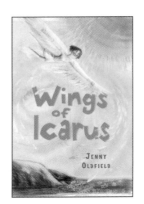

White Wolves Resources for Guided Reading

Year 4

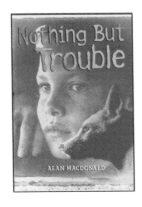

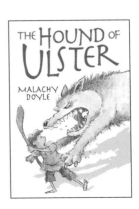

White Wolves Resources for Guided Reading

Year 5

Year 6

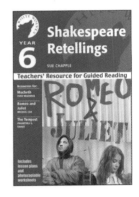

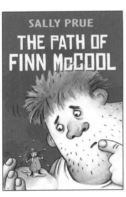

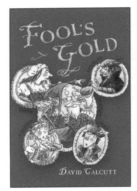

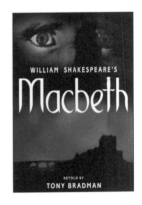

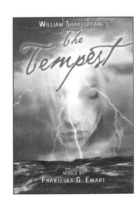